Activity Time

To my daughter Nicola Jane

Activity Time

A collection of creative activities for children

Compiled by
Sandra Sharp

JADE PUBLISHERS

HASLEMERE

Jade Publishers
15 Stoatley Rise
Haslemere
Surrey GU27 1AF

First published 1990

Cover and text illustrations by Alma Spriggs
Cover design by Samantha Edwards
Text design by Susan Harris

Typesetting by DP Photosetting, Aylesbury, Bucks

Printed and bound by Bocardo Press, Didcot.

British Library Cataloguing in Publication Data
Sharp, Sandra 1958 –
Activity time: a collection of creative activities for
children.
1. handicrafts for children
I. Title
745.5083

ISBN 0–903461–33–1

Contents

Introduction

Having worked for many years with young children, I appreciate the problem of constantly trying to think of different activities which will keep them occupied and happy whilst also broadening their knowledge and developing their skills.

Something I have often felt in need of is a good book to provide ideas. I especially needed help during my N.N.E.B. training. Therefore, I decided to collect together activities I have experienced myself and seen other people do, and write this book to help students, Nursery Nurses, Playgroup staff, teachers and mothers by providing a quick reference guide to ideas.

All the activities have been tried and tested. Most can be tackled easily by nursery age children with adult supervision, although some are aimed at older children. However, you will find that many activities are versatile and can be adapted for a different age range. Mothers at home with young children will be able to use many of the activities, depending on how much mess they can bear!

Of course, it is necessary to take great care when using any creative materials with small children, especially those involving scissors, needles or any other sharp and potentially dangerous objects.

I hope this collection is as helpful to you as it has been to me over the years, and I thank all my friends and colleagues for their inspiration and support during the compilation of this book.

SANDRA SHARP

Terms used in this book

Template

The shape or figure you require made from stiff card such as a butterfly or rabbit or even a simple shape such as a square or circle. A template enables the children to achieve a recognisable form which they would otherwise have difficulty in producing. Drawing round a shape and then cutting it out is an important skill for developing eye-to-hand co-ordination and hand control. Be prepared to help a child by steadying the template as he or she draws round.

Frieze

A large picture which often stretches along a display board. Very often many things are made by a group of children and then built up on the picture; for example, an Autumn frieze could have a bare tree, falling leaves, squirrel collecting nuts, and perhaps a child wearing warm clothes. Remember to keep friezes simple, with large, bright pictures and not too cluttered. Mount the picture at the children's eye level: they will not be interested in anything for long if they have to look up.

Mobile

Anyone who has had experience with babies will recognize this term. Quite simply, a mobile hangs from the ceiling and moves in the air currents – it is *mobile!* Various shapes and figures can be made to suspend from a mobile frame (see ideas on page 83), but remember three rather important points: as both sides of the shape will be on display, ensure that the children cover both sides; make the shapes from strong paper or card as the weight and movement will cause flimsy models to bend; suspend figures low enough for the children to see easily. This may be a nuisance for adults who will probably be constantly bumping into them, but, as with friezes, if a mobile is too high, children will totally ignore their work. As a guide, mobiles should hang just out of children's reach.

Activity

During the very early days of my training I can remember a teacher asking me to do an activity, and I had no idea what she meant. For those of you who may be in the same situation, a brief explanation may help. Generally speaking, if you are required to organize an activity, it will mean something creative – painting, printing, sticking or making a model, and this book will help you there. But do remember not all activities are creative ones. If you play a matching game with a group of children, this is also an activity, but a social and intellectual one. So occasionally offer to organize a sorting activity using buttons or weigh various classroom items in balancing scales. Both types of activity develop various skills and provide good basic pre-school education. Creative work can always follow on from such an activity, if required, in the form of paintings, drawings or perhaps a large frieze to illustrate it clearly.

Activities can be extended by using relevant rhymes, stories and so on. Some appropriate rhymes are given in this book.

You may find, especially if you are a student in a school, that you will be expected to organize an activity once a week.

Points to remember on creative activities

1   Always prepare activities well in advance, ready for the children to start as soon as they arrive.

2   Experiment yourself beforehand with different types of paper, so you know which will give the best effect.

3   Ensure the children are protected with suitable aprons.

4   Name each child's painting clearly and check correct spelling: many names are spelt unconventionally nowadays.

5   Always supervise well, encouraging language and development of skills. Be aware of safety and hygiene too.

6   Encourage the children to do the activity by themselves as far as possible. If you find that you are having to help a child too much, then the activity is too difficult and you should not be attempting it with that age range. A child will get absolutely nothing out of *watching* you make something: it is important to learn skills by practice.

7   Do not be tempted to neaten things or to tidy up pictures in order to make them recognizable. It does not matter that a circle which a child has attempted to cut out ends up misshapen: he or she will develop this skill in good time.

8   Vary activities to develop a good all-round sense of skills.

9   Have no more than four children at a time on an activity, depending on the degree of ability. Some children need individual help with cutting, for example, whereas others will cope competently. Remember: to teach children, you have to be relaxed and patient. If you have four children all demanding your attention at once, you will become harassed and no one will enjoy the activity or learn anything from it. Very often two children are quite enough!

10   Cover tables with newspaper as necessary.

11   Keep a good supply of materials in drawers and boxes for activities:

Drawers *(in a unit such as used for storing DIY nails, screws, etc)*	Boxes *(in a stock cupboard)*
assorted scraps useful for collage, e.g. pasta, etc (see also p. 43)	junk packets
wool	toilet roll tubes
shells	margarine tubs
buttons	yoghurt cartons
cards	felt
scraps of foil	fur fabric
scraps of tissue paper	wallpaper books
gummed paper	magazines
cotton reels	mail order catalogues
	fabric

Types of paper

Newsprint

A plain buff or white, thin, smooth paper which is inexpensive and generally used for painting at easels.

Sugar paper

A thicker, more textured paper available in a variety of bright colours and sizes. Tends to be absorbent.

Tissue paper

A very thin paper which is easily torn. Available in beautiful colours, but if money is scarce, collect the sheets used in bakeries to wrap bread. Good for sticking on to other paper. Particularly effective when the light shines through from behind, such as window pictures.

Crepe

A strong, stretchy type of paper. Has a variety of uses, such as hats or streamers for Christmas. Care must be taken to prevent crepe paper becoming wet, or its dye will run and stain.

Cartridge

Very good quality paper, thick, strong and expensive. Best kept for special pictures or occasion cards, like Christmas and Mother's Day.

Card

Many schools purchase large and small sheets of coloured card, but if these are unavailable due to expense, take a look in the larder at home: packets like tea bag boxes and icing sugar packs have lovely bright colours which may be usable. Card from cornflake packets also has many uses, so there is no need to spend out a great deal of money if you are prepared to improvise.

Gummed

Usually available in packets of various bright colours and different sizes. Gummed on the plain white side which only needs to be moistened to stick. Many children will be quite happy to lick the gummed side, but some may object to the taste, in which case provide a small pot of water and a paste brush.

Wallpaper

Most decorating shops are very obliging when asked for old sample books. Unwanted rolls of wallpaper can be cut into large sheets and used on the easels for a change or if money is scarce and newsprint not available.

Scrap

Again to save on expenditure, keep a box full of old paper which has only been used on one side: newsletters, advertising posters, old computer print-outs etc. These can then be used freely by the children for drawing and everyday activities.

Types of glue

Paper paste

There are several brands of paste for use with paper and light sticking which are now available from stationers and good toy shops.

P.V.A.

This is a stronger glue used for sticking collage, models and card. It is thick and white in appearance, and some brands dry clear so it can be used as a seal over pictures to give a glossy finish like varnish. It can also be mixed with powder paint for covering plastics such as washing-up liquid bottles, whereas powder paint on its own would flake off. Although there are several brands of P.V.A. on the market, only some state that they are washable, so as with all creative activities do ensure children's clothes and furniture are well covered. If clothes do get marked, sponge immediately with a little detergent on a damp cloth, and for dried-on stains rub in a little white spirit and wash thoroughly.

Flour-paste

Other than the commercial glues available, you can make a perfectly adequate paste for sticking paper from flour and water. Put 8 oz of flour and 1 teaspoon of salt into a pan and slowly add about 1 pt of water to make a smooth paste. Heat until it thickens (about 5 minutes) and then leave to cool. Store in the fridge.

Needless to say, superglue should **never** be used and neither should wallpaper paste as it contains a fungicide.

Types of paint

Powder paint

Can be purchased in various sized tins. The powder can be a little messy when mixing, so spoon it out carefully and protect your clothes: although many of the brands state that they are washable, in my experience some of the colours are very hard to remove. Bear this in mind when the children are painting. If clothes are marked, soak overnight in cold water and then wash in warm water and *hand soap* (not washing powder). This seems to be the best way to remove the paint, but it is not always totally successful. To make the paint: put 4 good tablespoons of powder into a non-spill paint pot and gradually mix in cold water to make a thick paste. Don't be tempted to use more water to get more paint – runny paint is a disaster both for the children to use and for you to clear up! Experiment by adding made-up paste instead of water and you should get a lovely thick paint which spreads smoothly.

Ready-mixed paint

Usually available in squeezy-type bottles in a variety of colours. It is a real boon as it is quick and fairly clean to prepare, but it does work out expensive if you organize painting daily with a number of children. This paint is very thick, so you may get away with watering it down a little, but again do not make it too thin.

When the painting session has finished, always wash the lids and brushes thoroughly to prevent the paint becoming dried-on and clogged. Children will not find painting inviting if the pots look messy. You can top up the paints during the week, but then clean out completely and make up fresh paint, otherwise the paint begins to smell.

Some other common paints available in schools are palette paints, tempera blocks, Colourets mixed with glycerine, and marbling paints which are oil-based.

Other materials

Dough

Method 1

This is an extremely long-life playdough that will last for months if kept in an airtight container, but it involves cooking. This can either be done by you at home or, even better, organize the children to help you if you are lucky enough to have some form of hotplate in a school or playgroup situation. Naturally, all actual cooking must be done by you.

3 cups plain flour
1½ cups salt
3 tablespoons cream of tartar

3 cups water
3 tablespoons oil
food colouring.

Put all ingredients into a saucepan. Stir over a low heat, beating until the mixture thickens and comes away from the sides of the pan to form a ball. Turn out on to a smooth surface and knead thoroughly when cool.

Method 2

A quick dough that needs no cooking.

½ lb–1 lb plain flour
a handful salt (to preserve dough)
or
Use self-raising flour and no salt for a stretchy, elastic dough.

Mix with water in a bowl to a smooth dough which is neither too dry nor too sticky.

Children love to imitate grown-ups making cakes. Moulding dough also promotes social play, allows emotions to be expressed, exercises the control of small muscles and teaches concepts of texture, size, properties and so on. Provide rolling pins, cutters, bun tins etc, but on occasions remove equipment and encourage children to use only their hands.

Clay

This is far more pleasant to use these days. It used to have to be made up from powder by mixing in water, which was very messy, but blocks of soft clay can now be bought and cut up with a cheese cutter to the required amount. For children to play with in a free situation, two cubes of about 15 cm square will suffice. However, if you want the children to make models you will need much more. To prevent the clay from drying out, and so that you can use the same lumps time and time again, follow this simple procedure:

1 Bang and shape the clay into two cubes.

2 Press a hole into the middle with your thumb.

3 Fill the holes with water.

4 Wrap the clay in a polythene bag and keep in a plastic bucket with a lid.

When the children use the clay, provide long aprons to cover them and put the clay on formica boards. They can use modelling knives (plastic ones) and their hands to shape the clay.

If making models to last: shape the clay (baskets are very simple to start off with) and then the results can be fired if you have access to a kiln, or baked in a very slow oven. When hard and cool, the models can be painted and kept for years.

A new type of clay, called Reinforced Modelling Clay, which will harden without having to be fired in a kiln, is now available from good quality toyshops. It hardens as it dries. Glaze and tools are also available as accessories.

Modelling clay, such as plasticine

Can be purchased in many bright colours. Again provide formica boards and encourage the use of hands for modelling. The more modelling clay is handled, the softer and easier to mould it becomes.

Bubbles

Provide washing-up bowl, made-up from children's bubble bath for each child, and fill large margarine tubs with soapy water. Put the tubs inside the bowls to collect spillage and let the children blow bubbles with clay pipes or straws. Cover the children with water aprons first!

Buttons/Shells (for sorting)

Put out a tray of buttons or shells and give the children little pots to sort different types into. This encourages language and mathematical skills, such as the concepts of large and small, colour, shape, shiny and so on. With very small children, watch they do not swallow such small objects.

Cornflour

An activity which fascinates children and adults alike. When mixed with water, cornflour has some amazing properties. Spread the mixture on to a formica surface and let the children play, using their fingers and spoons. They should discover the following things: although it looks runny, it is difficult to push; picked up on a spoon, it gradually *runs* off, although you would imagine it to drop off in a lump; it feels smooth and leaves your hands soft. Try it and see. A good project for older children is to discover what ingredient causes the strange effects.

Sand

Ordinary builder's sand stains yellow, so use silver sand purchased from educational suppliers, most toyshops and some builder's merchants. Special sand-pit sand is usually fine, but you may get a slight yellow staining when it is used wet for the first time.

Wet sand: Use things that will make forms, such as buckets and spades, jelly moulds.
Dry sand: Use things for pouring and filling such as sieves, cups, containers with holes.

Water

Fill a deep container with warm water. Washing-up liquid or food colourings may be added occasionally for interest. Use similar utensils as with dry sand, also things that float or sink, such as corks and stones, and absorbent items such as sponges.

Water and sand are both important for learning pre-maths skills such as volume, weight, full and empty.

Wendy House

A small corner arranged to resemble a mini house with toy furniture, tea set and dolls provides a lovely environment for imitation and imaginative play. A box of dressing-up clothes, hats and bags adds interest. Occasionally change the corner and accessories into different situations such as hospital, hairdressers, cafe, school etc.

Other items

Puzzles, construction toys, large bricks, books, music table, crayons and pencils are all a selection of activities which can be provided for the children every day.

Painting

Painting is extremely important in a child's development, in both free expression and organized activities. It develops hand-to-eye co-ordination, allows emotions to be expressed, and teaches colours and a sense of pattern and carefulness. It also provides a good basis for writing later on, as it helps to develop hand control and, of course (most important) *it's fun*.

Brushes are the most used utensils and come in different thicknesses; as well as ordinary children's paintbrushes, use toothbrushes, nail-brushes, household paint brushes, old hairbrushes and combs etc. for a change.

Try using different areas to paint on occasionally also, such as the floor, tables (cover both well with newspaper), directly on to a wall if possible, outside when sunny, in the bath or paddling pool (using body or face paints which easily wash off), and so on.

A very important factor in painting is to ensure that children are fully protected. Plastic slip-on aprons that the children can try to manage themselves are ideal for easel painting, but for messier activities (finger painting, for example) a boy's or man's shirt put on back to front and fastened down the back is good protection. Some paint and some glues are very difficult to remove from clothes, but this should not spoil children's enjoyment. If you are aware of any clothing showing, protect it.

Remember that children's paintings go through various stages of development, so it is not always just the representational ones that mean something. Try to display the scribble ones and the splodgy ones also – they are all very important to the young artist.

Below are descriptions of various types of painting activities.

Bubble painting

Mix pots of powder paint with water and a capful of children's bubble bath. Children blow through a drinking straw into the paint, causing bubbles to rise over the top of the pot. Sometimes a child will *suck* instead, so have plenty of drinking water handy! Taking a small sheet of paper, show the children how to lay it over the top of the pot and press down gently. The bubbles will print on to the paper and produce a gentle effect suitable for flowers or clouds on a frieze or simply as a pattern for the child to take home. Always remember to write each child's name clearly on his or her picture.

Blow painting

Make up fairly thin paint with water. Use a thick drinking straw so that the children can blow the paint easily. First they drop blobs of paint on to a smooth, thin paper and then blow the paint across the paper. Use a fresh straw for each child.

Splatter painting

Make up thin paint again and children simply flick on the paint with a paintbrush. Stand back!!

Pepperpot painting

Fill old pepper or spice pots with dry powder paint and shake on to wet paper. As the paint hits the paper, it appears to explode. Experiment to find your own best method of wetting the paper: I either immerse it in a tray of cold water or brush water over the paper with a thick paint brush (children can do this themselves). Either way, the paper must be thoroughly soaked to achieve the best effect.

Squeezy painting

Make up paint with glue and thin down with water. Then pour into old washing-up liquid bottles or bathroom cleanser bottles. Some hair-dressing preparations are sold in small squeezy-type bottles with long nozzles which are ideal for this activity. Children have great fun squirting the paint across the paper in long lines.

Spray painting

Make up thin paint once again and fill any type of old container which will spray, such as the all-purpose household sprays, window cleaners, or the small plastic bottles also used for hair lacquer. **Ensure all containers are thoroughly cleaned of all chemicals before being used.** Children simply spray the paint over the paper or you can make some cardboard stencils and pin them on to the paper. Then the children can spray over the shapes. Remove the templates to leave the shape unpainted on the paper.

Examples of templates

The above activities used in conjunction with one another produce a very effective bonfire picture as each gives the feel of explosion and colour.

Marble painting

Place a sheet of paper in an old tray or baking sheet. Drop a marble into a saucer of prepared thick paint and the children can roll the marble over the paper by tipping the tray from side to side. Mix the colours to achieve an effective picture.

Finger painting

Make up paint thickly with P.V.A. glue or paste and then drop about two spoonfuls of one colour on to a formica top or table. Let the children play about with the paint using their hands to spread it and make patterns. Encourage them to make a clear pattern or picture by using their fingers carefully. When they have drawn a picture they are satisfied with, take a print by laying a plain piece of paper over the pattern and pressing firmly over the back. Readymade finger paints can be purchased from good quality toy shops or art shops.

Dribble patterns

Make up four pots of thin paint. The children dribble the paint across the paper with a paint brush. Then picking the paper up, they make the paint run by tipping it various ways.

Wax resist or magic painting

Offer a smooth paper and tell the children to draw an invisible object or pattern with a white wax crayon or a candle. Then they paint over the picture with a *very thin* (almost a wash) coloured paint. The image originally drawn should appear, as if by magic, through the paint. NB. To achieve good results, the children do have to press very hard when drawing, so this activity may prove difficult for young nursery age children. If coloured wax crayons are used, the children can see what they are drawing and they can also see that the paint does not cover wax.

Marbling

An early experiment in Science to prove that oil and water don't mix! Make up various paints by mixing the powders with cooking oil instead of water (you'll only need a little). Fill an old roasting tin or large tray with water and then the children can drop a little paint, in different colours, on to the water, using a stick or the end of a paintbrush. The paint will float on the surface and the children can use the stick to break up the droplets and swirl the paint into patterns. Take a piece of good quality white paper (like cartridge), turn one of the corners over a little and crease. Use this corner to write on the child's name and then, holding the paper by the corner, lay on the surface of the water. Remove and place somewhere flat to dry. The result should be a beautiful marbled effect over the paper.

Special marbling paints can be bought from educational suppliers or art shops, which are ready to use and save making your own. Household paints are unsuitable: although oil-based, they will ruin clothes and are difficult to remove from hands.

large shallow tray filled with water

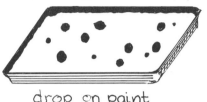 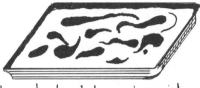

drop on paint   break droplets and swirl

fold corner back

write child's name on corner. (This is the only piece which won't be covered in paint)

lay paper on surface   example of finished picture
holding corner

Comb painting

Cut combs from stiff cardboard in several different designs as shown:

or use old haircombs
with some teeth removed   →

Apply some paint to the paper with a spoon and then the child combs the paint across the paper to make a pattern. Encourage the children to experiment by turning their hands various ways to achieve different results. This method gives an effect similar to 'Artex', and is excellent for sea pictures and friezes which require a wave effect.

Mirror painting

Fold a sheet of white newsprint in half widthways. Encourage the children to paint a pattern on *one half only* and then, before the paint dries, fold the paper over on the crease to produce a symmetrical pattern on the other half. Talk about reflections and mirror images, and introduce 'half' and 'whole'.

Butterflies

Use stronger paper (sugar paper is ideal) if you want to make butterflies that will suspend from mobiles. Fold the paper in half and ask the child to draw round a template you have made of half a butterfly, then get him or her to cut it out carefully, making sure the fold is not cut. Open out and you have a perfectly matched butterfly shape. Explain that butterflies have matching patterns and then proceed as for mirror painting. Use this activity within a project on the metamorphosis of the butterfly.

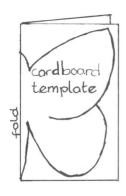

cut round template

cardboard template

fold

paint patterns on one side only and fold over to print

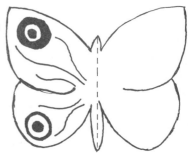

When both sides of the butterfly have been painted and dried, stick or staple a painted toilet roll tube down the centre and thread cotton through it to suspend. NB. If the butterflies don't hang correctly, thread some cotton through the top end of one wing, then through a cut piece of drinking straw, and finally out through the other wing. Tie off and attach another piece of cotton round the middle of the straw and hang from the ceiling. This should keep the wings up, but you will have to experiment to get it right.

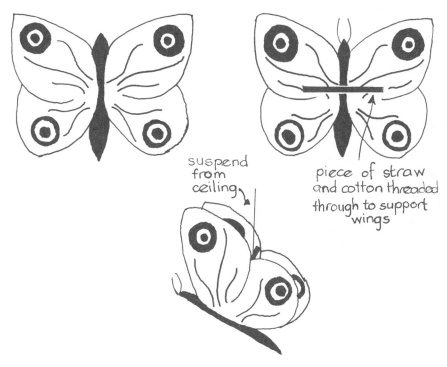

suspend from ceiling

piece of straw and cotton threaded through to support wings

String painting

Make up four colours of powder paint as usual (page 14) in large margarine tubs (500g size). Cut four long lengths of string and dip each one into a pot of the paint, so you have a blue string, green string and so on. Fold a sheet of strong sugar paper in half to make a crease and open out. Then the child chooses his or her first colour and places the painted string down the fold. The paper is folded and the child 'takes the string for a walk' by pulling it outwards and then upwards, holding the top of the string and the paper firmly. You may have to help with this. Open up the paper and see the lovely pattern it has produced.

You may find better results are achieved if you let each colour dry before applying the next, but this restricts the enjoyment the children get out of the activity, so try letting them apply a different colour immediately after the first whilst still wet and notice the effect as the colours mix.

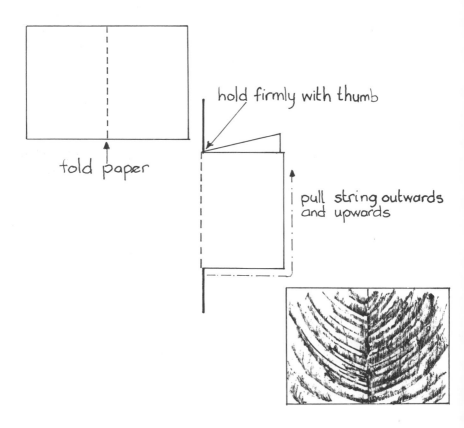

folded paper

hold firmly with thumb

pull string outwards and upwards

Printing

Just about anything can be used to print with as long as it has a good, clear texture. Some examples are listed below.

For all printing you need to begin with an old baking sheet or tray and cutting a piece of thin sponge to fit inside it. Use two trays if possible and make up two different colours of thick paint. Pour the whole pot of paint into the tray, allowing the sponge to soak it up. It is then ready for the children to use. They pick up the utensil they desire (see below), press it firmly into the paint and then print on to their piece of paper. Suggested printing utensils are cotton reels, lids, shells, fingers, hands, feet (this is an ideal summer activity if you have space outside for children to walk along a long roll of paper, and feet washing will be easier – compare feet sizes), toothbrushes, matchboxes, small cubes of sponge, balloons, bottle tops, lego, forks etcetera.

Potato prints

Cut a potato in half across the middle. Decide on a shape and mark it on the potato. Then cut away round the *outside*, leaving the shape protruding.

example of picture

Homemade blocks

Very simple blocks can be made by using cuboid or cube-shaped blocks of wood (approximately 12 cm × 16 cm × 4 cm). Onto one side of the block screw on a handle of some kind (pull-type door handle or knob) and on the other side stick on something that will make a clear print, such as string curled round, bottle tops, lego bricks, and so on.

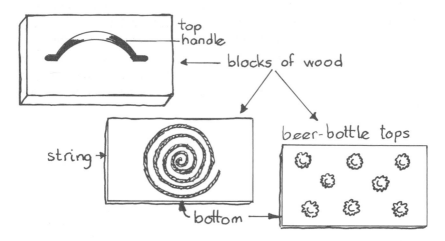

Leaf prints

Collect interesting leaves with the children, especially in Autumn with all its lovely colours. Although these can be printed with, also collect a few fresh, green pliable leaves as the dead leaves will probably crack. To print, the children press the leaves into the soaked sponge and then flatten them on to the paper with an old paint roller. This ensures a clear, even print. For a change, use material to print on (such as an old, cut up sheet). Neaten the edges and tie on wool to hang it up. This will make a lovely calendar for Christmas.

Rhyme

All the leaves are falling down
In Autumn colours of yellow and brown.
The wind it comes and blows them round
Into a heap upon the ground.

Balloon printing

Make up paint and pour into the trays. Blow up two balloons. Children can achieve a print by gently rolling a balloon in the paint and then on to the paper.

String prints

Prepare this activity as described for string painting (page 25). Provide plain white paper and four tubs of colour. Fold the paper in half and open again to crease. Then, instead of the child pulling the string out, he or she lays the paint-soaked piece of string on half the paper in a curly pattern and folds the other half of paper over the top. Press down lightly, open out, remove the string and repeat with other colours. This produces lovely bright prints.

Dishmop painting

If you can get hold of two old dishmops, they provide a lovely variation to paintbrushes. Provide two trays of paint (old baking trays are fine) and let the children wipe the mops in the paint and on to large pieces of paper.

Two-brush painting

Instead of using just one paintbrush all the time, why not encourage the use of two and let the children experiment for different results? If they hold the brushes firmly and have good hand control, they will see that the paint lines run parallel to each other. More able or older children will be able to space the brushes between their fingers and therefore space the lines; also they may be able to cope with three or four brushes at once.

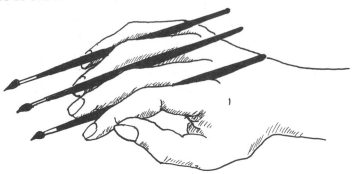

Frost patterns

Make up thick white paint with glue. Provide coloured or black sugar paper, and ask the children to cover the paper completely with the white paint. Then, using their fingers, they make patterns in the white paint (such as loops, twists and circles). Talk about frost and look at it on the windows on a really cold winter's day. See also **Snowflakes** on page 38 in the section on **Cutting and sticking**.

Rhyme

Jack Frost is here to chill the night
And everything turns from black to white.

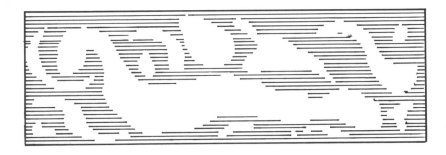

Doiley patterns

Buy two or three plastic doilies for the children to use. Plastic ones are more satisfactory than paper which will tear easily and have to be discarded. The doiley is used like a stencil. Fasten it lightly with sticky tape on to a sheet of paper and ask the child to paint over the doiley, covering all the holes. When the child removes the doiley, its pattern will be printed out on to the paper. Let the child use several colours over one doiley and also move the doiley to another space on the paper for another print. When it is dry, the child can cut round the patterns to produce a more interesting shape; this involves the child more in the activity.

Drawing and crayonning

Rubbings

Use thin, smooth paper, such as newsprint. Place the paper over anything with a textured finish. Suitable items are:

coins	tree bark
wire basket	walls
lego bricks	paving stones
stickle bricks	frosted glass windows
raffia mats	leaves

Have a selection of the smaller things on the table and talk about texture, using words like rough and smooth. Or use the activity outdoors on a fine day. Children must be encouraged to rub hard, using the *side* of a wax crayon, and keep the paper taut. Young children may need some help to control the crayon.

Templates

Using logic blocks or thick cardboard shapes you have made yourself (squares, triangles and so on), encourage children to arrange shapes to form a picture (such as a car or house). Then they draw the shapes to make the picture on their piece of paper. They can colour the picture in if they wish. This is an excellent shape lesson.

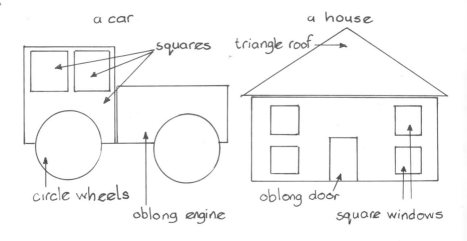

Faces

Fix a large mirror in front of a chair and table (perhaps resting it securely on a paint easel). Then seat each child in turn and talk about reflection and his or her features. The child can then reproduce his or her face on a large sheet of paper with the correct colouring. You could follow up this activity by getting the children to study each other and then draw full length pictures including ears, shoulders, legs, etc. (Many three to four-year olds are at the stage of progressing from drawing 'arms out of heads' and 'no bodies' to more accurate pictures. So, when you think they have reached this stage of development, this activity is a good teaching aid. Good questions are: How many legs, arms, etcetera?

Sand pictures

Encourage children to draw pictures or shapes in sand with sticks or fingers. This is ideal for beach activities or in a large sand pit. Alternatively, spread wet sand over a large plastic sheet outside on the ground, or give each child its own sand tray (simply spread a shallow layer of sand over an old lunch tray).

Wax scratch

Children crayon completely over a sheet of paper. Then let them use a sharp point of a pencil or the end of a paint brush to scratch a picture in the wax. Take care of sharp points, teaching children to realise such dangers and use things properly, whether scissors or any sharp instrument.

Chalk pictures

Using black or coloured sugar paper, let the children use chalks instead of crayons to draw their pictures. Coloured chalks can be very messy, so aprons should be worn.

Cutting and sticking

The nursery is very often the place where many children learn to cut; indeed, it may be the first time any of them have even experienced the handling of scissors. Many parents are, understandably, very fearful of allowing children to cut at home. However, I feel, along with many others, that if children are taught how to use scissors properly and to understand the dangers, and then allowed to cut freely *only what they are given to cut* and *not* their clothes, hair or furniture, they will not be tempted to experiment when they are out of sight – which, of course, could be extremely dangerous. The old story of the forbidden fruit is very true in many cases.

Teaching a child to cut is no easy task as those of you who have tried will, I am sure, agree. Children love to cut once they find it easy, but they just won't try if it is made hard for them. Therefore, provide *sharp* round-ended scissors and thin paper. Blunt scissors will only cause frustration and you will achieve nothing.

The basic rules you should impress on the children are:

1   Never walk round the room with scissors in your hand.

2   Never wave scissors about.

3   Never put scissors up to or in your mouth.

4   *Paper* is for cutting, *not* clothes, hair or books!

5   Hold scissors properly with fingers in the correct holes.

6   Never use mummy's, daddy's or teacher's 'big' scissors (but if children have their own scissors, they probably won't want to).

Cutting is a skill that has to be learnt and it is very satisfying when it is finally achieved, both for the teacher and for the child. Plenty of practice is the only way, so most days provide a table for cutting on with lots of colourful pages from magazines and catalogues so that the children can just keep cutting unaided but supervised. If you make little bags from scrap paper folded and stapled with their name on, the children can keep their cuttings and take them home in the bag.

For left-handed children, cutting is extra hard; however, scissors specially designed for such children are now available to make life a little easier.

Occasionally you can organise the cutting into activities like the following ones.

Greeting card pictures

Collect old Christmas cards, birthday cards, etcetera and tear off their backs to make it easier for the children to cut out figures or objects. Then stick the cut-outs on to pieces of paper with flour and water paste. Large pieces of newsprint or sugar paper are ideal for such backgrounds. Sometimes encourage the children to look carefully at the card they have chosen and to pick out a figure, bell or robin to cut out. Then draw around the shape in a clear black pen and ask the child to try to cut on the line.

Wallpaper pictures

Tear out pages from old sample books (obtainable from decorators' shops). Choose bright, colourful wallpaper, and again encourage the children to cut round shapes, flowers and so on, and then arrange them on to their sheet of background paper.

Magazine collages

Tear out pages from old colour magazines and ask the children to cut out pictures they like. Again, help them by drawing round the shape if necessary. Very effective colour pictures can be produced by concentrating only on one particular colour: 'Let's find lots of blue things and stick them on a blue background.' Stick all the different shades of blue on the paper overlapping each other.

Tissue paper pictures

A good activity to demonstrate colour mixing. The children have to be very careful when cutting tissue as it tears so easily. When different shapes in different colours have been cut, the children can stick them carefully on to plain white paper with flour and water paste, overlapping two colours to make a third: for example, if a square of yellow overlaps a square of red, the piece in the middle will be orange. You could follow up this activity with colour-mixing paints and letting the children use orange, mauve and pink paints for a change. Make sure the children know their primary colours well first so as not to confuse them.

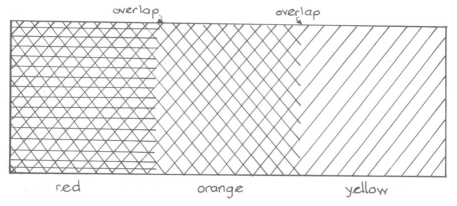

Stained glass windows

Fold a square of paper lengthways and then ask the child to draw round a template you have made of *half* an object such as a flower. Then cut out the shape. When the paper is unfolded, you will have a square of background paper with the shape cut from the middle.

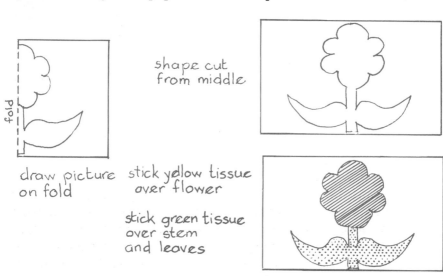

Then the child sticks on to the back of the paper a square of tissue paper to cover the hole. The picture shows up effectively when stuck on to the window and the light shines through it. Autumn leaves, Christmas things, toys, shapes all make good stained glass pictures.

Black on white or white on black?

Start with either a square of white paper or a square of black paper and ask the children to cut out various abstract shapes from the opposite colour and stick them on to the background piece. This results in a very effective picture which is hard to distinguish whether it started as white paper or black.

Silhouettes

From black paper the children cut shapes from templates you have made of ships, cars, houses, animals and stick them on to paper. These are effective for a large frieze. For a sea picture: paint the background with a pale blue wash and allow to dry; then stick on shapes of black boats.

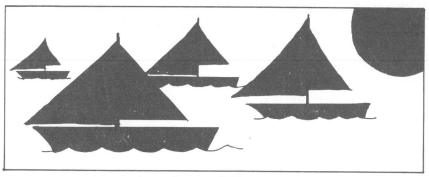

a sunset picture of the sea

String pictures

Cut off a length of string for each child; then, using strong P.V.A. type glue, which is white and easily seen and dries clear, they can make patterns on strong paper. When they have finished glueing, they then stick on the length of string in patterns, such as spirals, circles and so on. Older children will produce more controlled results – houses or animals can look very effective.

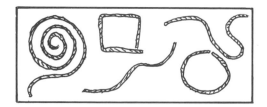

you can cut the string to each child's individual height and then make a picture from it

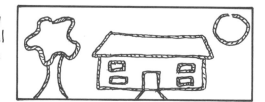

Flower pictures

Flower catalogues are easy to obtain. Tear out a few pages to make it easier for the children to cut. Encourage them to cut carefully round flowers and stick them on to bright sugar paper. These pictures are lovely to make at Springtime and look very effective.

Snowflakes 1

The children draw round a margarine tub to make a circle on white paper. Help them to fold the cut out circle in half, in half again and in half a third time if possible (although this third fold may make it too difficult for young children to cut; if so, only fold twice). Draw a pattern on to the triangle shape you have made and shade in; then ask the child to cut this piece out. Open up and there is the snowflake.

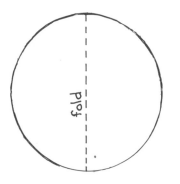

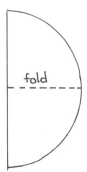

cut out shaded area

Snowflakes 2

Another method of making snowflakes is to fold a square of white
paper in half and half again, and then fold it diagonally to form a
triangle. Draw loops and half-circles on the folds and ask the children
to cut the bits out. Open out and either stick on black paper or suspend
on strings up at the windows. If the children stick a square of coloured
tissue on to the back of the snowflake, a lovely stained glass effect is
achieved when held up at the window.

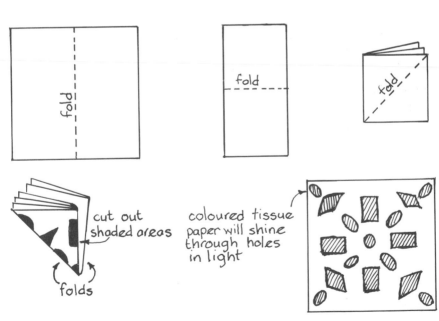

fold

fold

fold

cut out shaded areas

folds

coloured tissue paper will shine through holes in light

Paper necklace

Roll a length of newsprint paper loosely round a pencil and stick the edge down. Slide the pencil out to form a hollow paper tube (children will be able to do this with help).

Then they can cut the tube into ½ inch (2 cm) lengths and paint the lengths in different colours. When these are dry, provide strong thread or threading cord and ask the children to thread on the paper beads. Or cut up drinking/art straws, paint and thread.

Egg-box pictures

Egg boxes are very versatile and many different pictures can be made with them. A large dragon or crocodile is easy because you only have to draw a very rough outline and the children can fill in the shape with stuck-on egg boxes and paint it once dry. The egg cups from the boxes also make very good flowers with pipecleaners for stems (see also page 90). A lovely tortoise can be made from egg boxes and then painted carefully in brown and black to emphasize the pattern on his shell.

Conker line

When the children inundate you with conkers in the autumn, make good use of them and ask the children to stick them on to paper in a long line with strong P.V.A. glue. Or have individual lines and see who has collected the most conkers and made the longest line. You could turn this into a project on numbers and make a simple chart to introduce the children to graphs. The children could also make conker faces or houses.

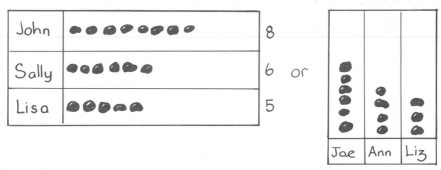

Eggshell pictures

Collect eggshells and wash carefully so they don't smell. Then ask the children to help you to crush them up by placing the shells in a paper bag and flattening with a rolling pin. Stick the results on to strong paper or card. Ideal for Easter pictures: chick hatching from an egg, for example.

Newspaper pictures

Children also love to tear as well as cut (as many parents with wallpaper torn off walls know very well!) So why not let them tear old newspaper (not the one mummy or daddy wants to read!) and make it clear that this is the only time they should *ever* tear paper, and *never* books or wallpaper. Pictures can be made either by getting the children to stick their torn pieces on to background paper in an abstract way or by first drawing an outline of an animal with a template and then sticking the newspaper inside the shape. Emphasise the animal by outlining it in black pen afterwards. Older children will be able to cope with representational pictures more than nursery age will.

Fabric pictures

Use old sheeting instead of paper and cut it into large squares for the children to stick on scraps of brightly coloured fabric. Sort out pieces of fabric which can be easily cut: felt, cotton and so on. Again, you can sometimes encourage representational pictures, such as people they can 'dress', but lovely pictures can be achieved by just allowing the children to do their own thing. Either way is valuable, but the important thing to remember is always to let the children do as much of the work as they possibly can by themselves and not *always* to make representational pictures, nor *always* let them have a totally free head, but find a happy balance in between.

Mosaics

The children can draw round a template of an object, such as a figure or easy shape, and then fill the shape by sticking on small squares of sticky paper (gummed one side which only needs to be licked; however, some children do not like the taste so you could provide a small tub of water and a brush). Encourage the children to stick the squares close together and not to leave gaps. You may find this is a little too difficult for very young children, but six to seven-year-olds will be able to cope more easily. A mosaic on a large scale, with bigger squares, or perhaps a frieze, is ideal for nursery age.

Collages

Keep a selection of various items in separate containers (such as old tobacco tins or mousse containers) in a drawer or box:

pasta	bus tickets	buttons	bottle tops
cereals	stones	lentils	(milk and beer)
matchsticks	sticks	leaves	string
egg shells	shells	wood shavings	lace
wool	tea leaves	dried peas	scraps of paper
sand	silver paper	beads	and fabric
matchboxes	seeds		

The above selection are all good collage material. Some items like shells and fabric you will need to keep in separate boxes as you will collect large amounts.

The children need to use a strong artist's medium glue (P.V.A. type) and strong paper, sugar or card to make their pictures. Lovely pictures are produced if the children are given a free hand to stick a selection of bits on to the background material.

Collage pictures also make effective friezes, for example, a fish from shells, people with fabric scraps for clothes, or a seaside picture with sand, shells and pebbles.

Tea trails

Save used tea bags and remove the tea when dry. When you have collected a fair amount, very effective pictures can be produced if the tea leaves are sprinkled on to a trail of strong glue. Lift up paper and shake gently to remove excess tea leaves.

Sand paintings

Adopt the same method as for tea trails but use sand instead. A variation is to mix the dry sand with dry powder paint and then the children sprinkle this on to large dollops of P.V.A. glue. Use *strong* paper (sugar paper or card) as sand is very heavy.

Straw pictures

Collect different sorts of drinking/art straws: plain, coloured, striped. Children can make very interesting pictures by sticking the straws in straight lines: patterns, houses, stick people, etcetera. Use strong glue. When dry, the pictures can be lightly painted if desired.

Button pictures

Children love sorting buttons, so keep a whole drawerfull just for playing with. Encourage the children to look carefully at the differences between individual buttons. Pictures can be made in connection with a shape project, such as a circle man or a ball. Collect other circular objects which can be used to make circle pictures (bottle tops, lids, etcetera).

Making models from junk

Good models can be made from old cereal packets, boxes, cake boxes, tea packets, toilet roll tubes, egg boxes, yoghurt pots and so on. The children need to use strong P.V.A. type glue; cover tables with newspaper and protect clothes with aprons. Supervise the children well and encourage the model-making. Sometimes themes can be given to this activity, for example, animals, the funfair, transport (cars, boats), etcetera.

Castle

Compile from four cornflake boxes. Draw various lines for the children to cut away parts of the boxes to resemble a castle. Draw a template of a square and get the children to draw round and cut out squares for bricks or stones, colour them in and stick on to the castle.

this is a castle of squares
who lives there?
who dares climb the square
stairs to see who lives in
the castle of squares

or

paper bricks

use eggbox tray to make a wall picture of a castle (the egg cups look like stone) cut to shape and paint towers made from paper squares

Rhyme

Who lives in this castle of squares?
Is it a giant, or a princess fair?
Shall we climb the steep, winding stairs
To see who lives in the castle of squares?

Train

For the carriages, use cuboid boxes of similar sizes (tissue boxes, for example), and a long thin cuboid for the engine with a toilet roll inner for the funnel. Stick two egg cups together for wheels. The children can stick all the engine boxes together with strong glue, cut out windows in the carriages, draw people on card and cut them out to fix behind the windows. Join the carriages together by poking pipe-cleaners through the boxes and bending them round.

Individual trains can be made from smaller boxes and then personalized with each letter of the child's name on a different carriage – a good way of encouraging children to learn their names. This idea can also be adapted into a form of wall picture or frieze on paper, or to fix on to the child's bedroom door at home. Remember to ask the child to write the letters; you can help by lightly forming the letters first and then getting him or her to copy over the top in bold pen.

track can be made from straws

Rhyme

Down at the station, early in the morning
Look at all the trains standing in a row.
Here come the passengers, sleepy and yawning,
Collecting their tickets, and off they go.

Happy witch

Cut a semi-circle from card and ask the children to use this as a template to draw and cut out the witch's body. Fold the shape round to form a cone and fasten with staples. Pierce holes in sides for arms.

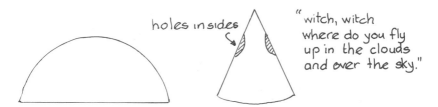

holes in sides

" witch, witch
where do you fly
up in the clouds
and over the sky."

Tie two straws together by bending one over the other held
horizontally and fasten with sticky tape.

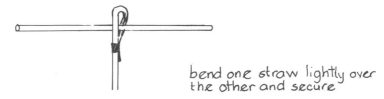

bend one straw lightly over
the other and secure

The horizontal straw is for the witch's arms and the vertical one is for
the stem. Get the children to push the straws up inside the cone; each
straw for the arms goes through the holes either side. Hands can be
made from black paper. The children can draw a face on a circle of
white paper and then stick it on to the body. Provide a jam-jar lid and
a smaller circle shape for the children to draw round on black paper,
one inside the other. Then fold the paper in half and ask the children
to cut along the lines to make a rim of a hat. This rim then fits over the
point of the cone to form the complete hat.

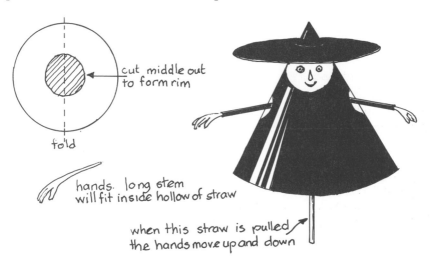

cut middle out
to form rim

fold

hands. long stem
will fit inside hollow of straw

when this straw is pulled
the hands move up and down

Rhyme

'Who's that, up there in the sky?'
'Where? In the clouds?'
'No, in the stars so high.'
'Oh! It's the happy witch, learning to fly.'

Always keep Hallowe'en very light and fun as young children can be very frightened by some of its concepts.

Rockets

Children colour toilet roll inners with bright paint and, when these are dry, they can stick on scraps of shiny foil paper and tissue paper. Then they can cut long strips of tissue paper and stick them to the bottom of the toilet roll to represent sparks. Finally, the children can cut an egg cup from an egg box, paint it and stick it on to the top of the toilet roll tube. Fix the whole rocket to a lolly stick or similar.

Catherine wheels

Firstly get the children to cut out a circle from coloured foil or other bright paper. On this you draw a simple spiral pattern and they can try carefully to cut round the line. Attach the middle of the spiral to a straw with a paper fastener so the wheel will spin.

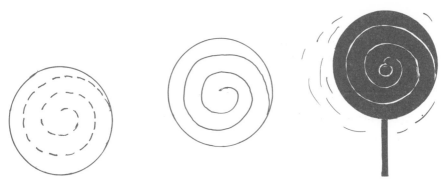

Simple sparklers

Collect toffee apple sticks or similar and the children can cut lengths of coloured tissue paper and stick them on to one end. Secure with a band of paper stuck down to hold the streamers on.

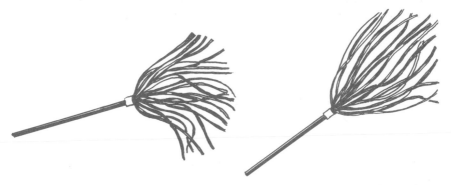

Bonfire night is fun but can be dangerous, so emphasize the safety rules.

Spiders

Use scraps of black fur fabric and provide a circular template for the children to draw round with white chalk on the wrong side of the fabric. When cutting the fur, they may need help. Then they can stick eight pipecleaners on for legs, securing them with staples, and add shiny paper or beads for eyes. Sew on shirring elastic to hang the spider so it bounces up and down.

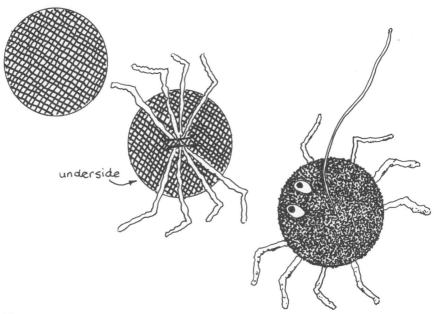

underside

Frogs

Make a template from card as shown and then cut the frog shape from polystyrene tiles. Young children may have difficulty cutting polystyrene so they could make their frogs from card. The shape is painted green, leaving the two eyes blank to be painted bright yellow later when the green is dry (or circles of bright yellow gummed paper stuck on).

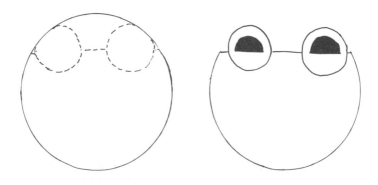

Rhyme

Five green frogs sitting by the pool,
One fell in! and it was nice and cool.
'Come on, my friends, come on in,
Join me for a long cool swim'.
Repeat 4, 3, 2, 1, and end the last verse. . . .
No more friends to join the fun,
so they all hopped out to sit in the sun.

Vase

A very simple vase can be made by cutting the top off of a washing-up liquid bottle and drawing an oblong of paper big enough to cover the writing. Then ask the children to cut this out. They can decorate by colouring, or sticking on flower pictures. Then the decorated oblong is stuck round the bottle. Put some stones in the bottom to weight the vase down. Makes a lovely present if you also add some flowers made by the children – see page 90.

Cotton reel animals

Snake: Collect quite a few cotton reels and ask the children to paint them (if you mix powder paint with a little P.V.A. glue, the paint will not peel off the cotton reel). When the paint is dry, the children can thread the reels on to a long thread or wool fastened at one end and then draw a face for the other end, as well as a long forked tongue.

Caterpillar: Attach two short lengths of pipecleaner for antennae. Encourage the children to paint a pattern on the finished creature.

Cat: Use a cotton reel for the body, and make one template for the face and front legs and another for the back legs and tail. Ask the children to draw round the templates and cut out. Then stick the features on to the body as follows:

Other animals such as a rabbit, donkey and so on, can also be made this way.

Binoculars

Ask the children to crayon two toilet roll inners, fasten them together with sticky tape and add a length of wool to hang round the neck. Talk about sight.

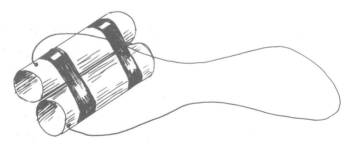

Telephone

The children can decorate two golden syrup tins for each telephone, with an oblong of coloured gummed paper (they can draw round a template and cut this out for themselves). You make a small hole in the bottom of each tin with a metal punch or similar tool. Then the children can help you to thread through a long piece of string (up to about 10 ft) and tie a secure knot inside each tin. It's very important to pull the phone tight between the two children using it; if this is done correctly, the one who listens will hear a very clear message through the tin. Talk about hearing and deafness.

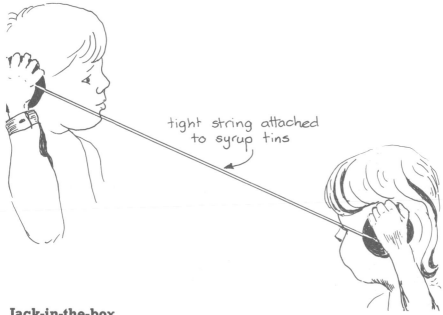

tight string attached to syrup tins

Jack-in-the-box

Ask the children to decorate a yoghurt pot by either painting it (mix the paint with P.V.A. glue) or by cutting out an oblong of paper and sticking on little shapes of gummed paper. Then from a template which you have made, they can draw and cut Jack out of paper and colour. Stick him on to a lolly stick and make a hole in the bottom of the pot. When Jack is pulled down by the stick, he should completely disappear into the pot and pop up again when the stick is pushed up.

Rhyme

Jack is a funny little man,
Hides in his box as still as he can.
Don't disturb, or lift the top,
Because UP HE'LL POP!

yoghurt pot

slit base

lolly stick

Bee

Make a template of the basic shape as shown:

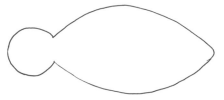

Children can colour this yellow and black, and then cut out two wings as shown.

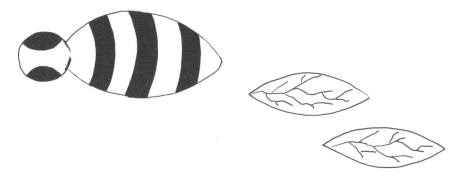

The eyes should be very large and coloured black.

The completed bee is then stuck to a toilet roll rube and pinned to the wall.

toilet roll inner

Egg box animals

Very young children may need help when cutting eggboxes.

Tortoise

Use a half-dozen size egg box and push in the two middle segments on the base to form four stubby legs. Another egg segment is used for the head and a cut-out paper shape for the tail. The pattern on the shell can be carefully drawn with a felt-tip pen, or the box can be painted brown all over and when dry the markings crayoned on.

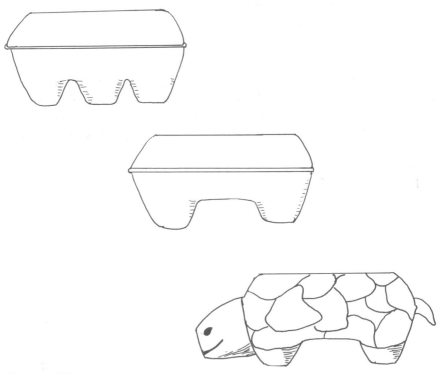

Caterpillar

Cut strips from large (2½ dozen size) egg trays (obtainable from markets or farms) and then the children can paint them all one colour. When the trays are dry, the children can carefully paint on a pattern.

Rhyme

Here comes the caterpillar, creeping, creeping.
Look at him now – he's sleeping, sleeping.
When he wakes and opens his eyes,
He'll be a butterfly, flying high.

Wasp or Bee

Use three segments of eggbox still joined in a row. Draw a shape of a wing on paper and ask the children to cut out two of these. The wings are stuck on either side of the middle segment and a pipecleaner or straw used for the antennae and sting. The body is painted black with yellow stripes.

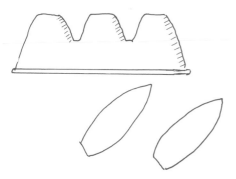

Rhyme

Look at the busy, busy bee,
busy all day long.
Listen to the busy, busy bee
singing his buzzing song – Buzz z z z z.

Snail

Cut out two segments of egg box still joined together and two separate ones. Stick the two separate ones, one on top of the other, on the second segments of the two joined together, so a high shell is formed. Thread a straw or pipecleaner through the head and stick on a cardboard tail. Paint any colour – pink, blue and yellow snails are lovely!

Owls

Use a paper plate, or draw and cut a circle of stiff card. The children can paint this brown and stick on milk bottle tops for eyes and cut-out triangles of paper for beak and ears.

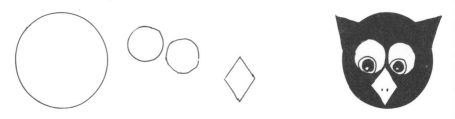

Making models from papier mâché

This is a very long process and one you will probably find unsuitable for very young children, but it does produce a substance with a lovely pliable consistency for moulding models. When dry, they can be painted and last a long time.

Process: Children can help you to tear up a great deal of newspaper into postage stamp sized pieces and then put it into a bucket of flour and water paste until the consistency is thick. Leave to soak and then drain away excess paste. The pulp remaining is then ready to use. Some children find the texture distasteful, but others love to squelch their hands into the mixture. However, it takes a great amount of newspaper and glue built up in many layers to achieve any sort of result, which takes a long time, so older children of six or seven will enjoy this more.

Paper mâché is ideal for making fruit (bananas, oranges, etcetera) for a pretend shop; animals (snakes, cats, rabbits) are also easy to mould. Paper mâché is also excellent for covering a mould of some kind to retain a shape: for example, a head for a model can be achieved by smoothing layers of newspaper and glue over a blown-up balloon; when these are dry and hard, burst the balloon and the head will remain intact.

Owl

Blow up a balloon and knot the end. Smear the whole balloon with petroleum jelly and cover with layers of papier mâché as previously described. When dry, burst the balloon. Fill the shell with something to make it stand upright (such as sand or dried peas). Paint it white or light brown, and then paint or make the owl's face. Stick on two egg box sections for ears.

Father Christmas

Use the balloon again and paint as before, or finish the last layer of the papier mâché with white paper. The children can draw on a face and add features like a cotton wool beard, moustache and eyebrows. The hat can be made from an oblong of red tissue stuck to the forehead and gathered to a bobble of cotton wool.

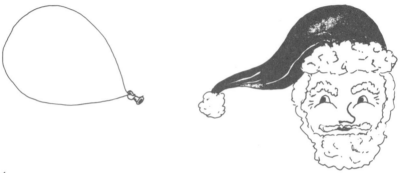

Cat

The balloon is used again and the features of a cat are easily painted on by young children. Make ears from egg cup segments and whiskers from pipecleaners.

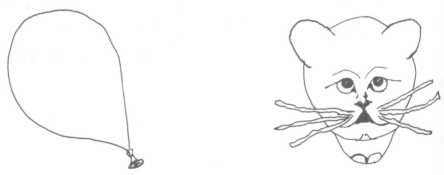

Egg

This time use an oval balloon. When the papier mâché is dry, the children can decorate it with bright colours. Then **you** can cut it in half with a Stanley knife, serrating the edge. This will look like an Easter egg breaking in half. Another idea is to let the children use broken and crushed eggshells to cover as the top layer of the egg and to make a fluffy chick (p. 84) to emerge from the broken pieces of egg.

Vase

This will be a vase for paper flowers only. Use an empty lemonade bottle (plastic to eliminate danger of smashing) and smear the lower half with petroleum jelly. Cover with papier mâché and remove the bottle when dry. Trim the top of vase to neaten. Paint the papier mâché a bright colour, or cover it with white paper and stick on scraps of pretty paper. Remember the vase won't hold water! See page 90 for flowers the children can make.

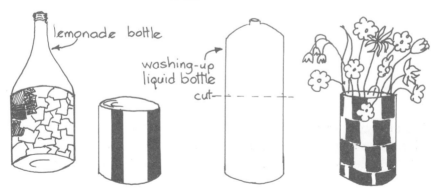

Puppets

Wallpaper puppets

Let children choose from bright wallpaper and then fold the chosen sheet in half so it is big enough to get two pieces (a back and a front) each the size of the child's hand. Ask the children to place their hands on the plain sides of the wallpaper and to draw round each hand leaving a two-inch margin. Cut out the hand shapes. Turn the wrong sides together and staple round the edge, leaving the bottom open for the hand to go in. Alternatively, you can use a hole punch and punch round the edge so the children can thread a large bodkin and wool through to join the back to the front (this takes more time, but is very effective and makes a very good hand control exercise for the children). Once the puppets are made, the children can decorate them with features and hair of paper and wool to make clowns, people, cats, and so on.

Yoghurt pot puppets

Invert the pot and ask the child to stick a Smartie tube or similar inside. This provides a strong handle when it is dry. Then ask the child to draw round an oblong shape on to white newsprint and cut it out. Stick this on to the yoghurt pot to provide a suitable surface for the child to draw on features. Add hair, hats, etcetera, offering ideas for a policeman, a clown, a cat, a girl and so on.

Plate puppets

Collect paper plates. The circular shape obviously suggests a face and, painted or decorated with scraps or materials, they are very easy to work with. Once the children have finished making the faces, attach the plates to lengths of dowling with very strong glue. You may have to give additional security by threading wool through the plate and sewing on the stick.

Sock puppets

Collect old, *washed*, socks and lots of scraps of fabric, paper and buttons. Puppets of dragons, crocodiles, giraffes, rabbits and so on can all be produced very effectively with careful thought. Put the sock on to your own hand so the child can see where the eyes, mouth and any characteristic marks should go. These features are made from suitable scraps and stuck on.

Finger puppets 1

Use a toilet roll tube and ask the children either to paint it or cut a square of paper to wrap round the tube and stick on. Then they can draw a face on a separate piece of paper, cut it out to stick on to the top of the tube and add any other features, hats, beard, etcetera. The children can put their fingers up inside the tube to make the puppet work.

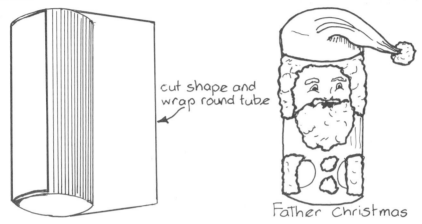

cut shape and wrap round tube

Father Christmas

Finger puppets 2

Cut various templates of easily-shaped animals and the children can choose one to cut out of thin card. Cut two holes for the fingers to go through and the children can colour accordingly.

Rhyme

Using names of appropriate puppets such as dogs, cats, ladies, and so on, you can adapt this rhyme:

Two funny clowns met in the street.
'Well, this is a funny place to meet.'
'I'm going to the circus for my tea,
Why don't you come along with me?'

Paper bag puppets

Collect large paper bags (plain white or brown are best), enough for each child to have one. These the children can decorate in any way they wish, sticking on wool, milk bottle tops, coloured sticky paper, straws and so on for features.

Remember to turn the bag upside-down before the child starts placing features, to form the puppet:

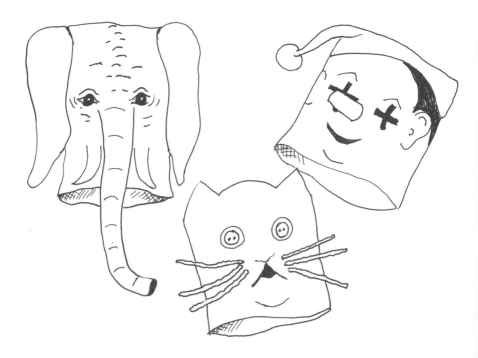

Obviously, if the children cut away the seam of the bag, it will have to be rejoined either with glue, staples or sticky tape.

These puppets can be varied very easily by cutting out suitable scrap pieces and sticking on to make distinctive features as shown:

Rhyme

An elephant is a huge grey lump.
His great big feet go thump, thump, thump.
He doesn't have fingers, he doesn't have toes,
But look at that trunk – Cor! What a nose?

Rabbit puppets

Make a fairly large template of a rabbit, without the ears, and ask the children to draw round it and cut out the shape. Then they can colour it with felt tip pens and add whiskers from drinking straws. You may have to help them cut out small circles for eyes. An easy way to cut circles is to fold the paper or card in half and then even a very young child should be able to cut carefully on the line from the fold *under supervision*.

The child's fingers become the rabbit's ears.

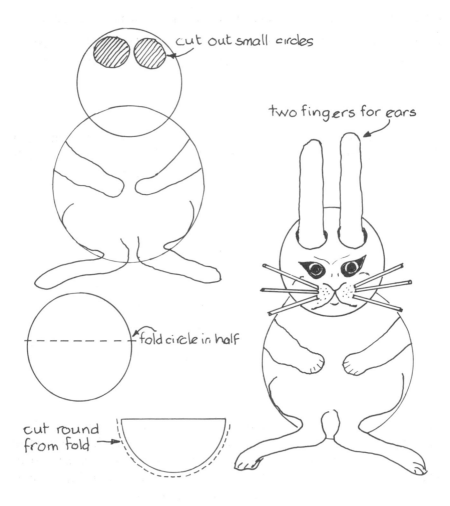

cut out small circles

two fingers for ears

fold circle in half

cut round from fold

Masks

All measurements for hats and masks will vary for different ages.

When fastening with staples, make sure you staple from the inside so the sharp ends are on the outside and not going to scratch the child's face.

Bandit masks

Make a template from card of two eyes and a long strip to go round the child's head. The children use the template to draw the mask on to stiff paper or card, and then cut it out. Colour or paint brightly.

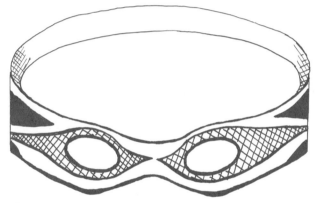

Paper sack

Buy paper refuse sacks (often green) from hardware shops, or collect packing bags from mail order catalogues. Turn upside down and fit on to the child to locate eyes (you may have to cut more off the bottom of the sack). Mark eyes and cut them out. Children can then have a free hand with decoration, sticking on scraps or painting.

You may find some children will refuse to put a sack completely over their heads. On no account should they be forced if they are afraid, but compromise by cutting away the back and fixing it with elastic or a strip of paper. Then this does not exclude the child from the activity.

REMEMBER NEVER TO USE PLASTIC BAGS, CHILDREN CAN EASILY SUFFOCATE INSIDE THEM.

Butterflies

Using strong paper, the children make butterfly prints as in the painting section (p. 24). When the paint is dry, hold the butterfly up to the child's face and mark where his or her eyes are and cut them out. Then attach elastic *through* the wings so as not to pull the mask back.

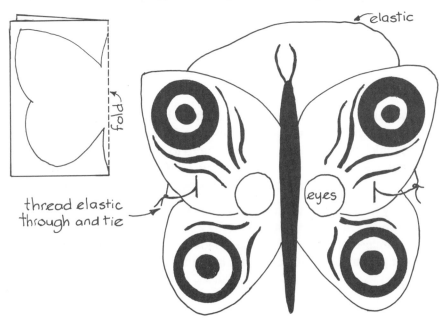

elastic

fold

thread elastic through and tie

eyes

Father Christmas

Make a simple template of a face and then the children can draw and cut out the shape. Talk about Father Christmas's beard, moustache and eyebrows and ask them to add these features with cotton wool. Make a hat as explained in the hat section (page 77), and to complete the simple outfit they could make a sack to *carry* from a large paper refuse sack decorated brightly and threaded with string to draw up round the neck (they could use this to take home the many things they make at school at Christmas time).

Egg box masks

Using a half-dozen size egg box, cut away the bottom outside two segments and push in the top middle segment as shown:

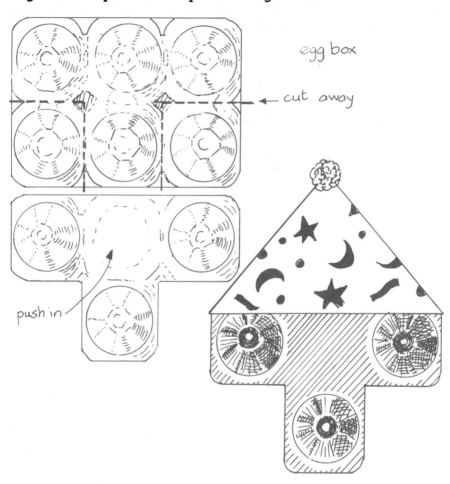

egg box

cut away

push in

Then the mask can be painted in any colour. If the children add a cone-shaped hat, made as shown in the hat section (page 79), the mask can easily be transformed into a clown.

Very simple quick masks can be made by cutting out two adjoining segments of an eggbox, making holes in their tips to see out of, painting them brightly and threading elastic from side to side.

Paper plate masks

These are made in a similar way to the puppets made from plates (page 64), but obviously *you* have to cut holes for the children's eyes and attach elastic. Alternatively keep the dowelling sticks instead of tying on, and then the children will hold the masks up to their faces.

Rocket masks

Make a template from card as shown and ask the children to cut out one each. Measure where the eyeholes go and cut them out. Then the children can stick on bright scraps of coloured foil, tissue and sticky paper. At the bottom long strips of tissue paper are added to give the appearance of flames. Fix the mask with a wide strip of strong paper long enough to go around the child's head and fastened either side of the rocket with staples.

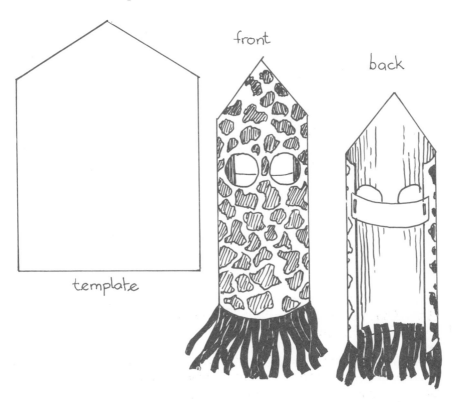

template

front

back

Tribal masks

Collect large plastic containers (the catering size of orange squash or detergent) and remove the top half with sharp scissors. If you look down on the top of the container, you will see the basic shape for the mask: the handle becomes the nose, the cap becomes the mouth and so on.

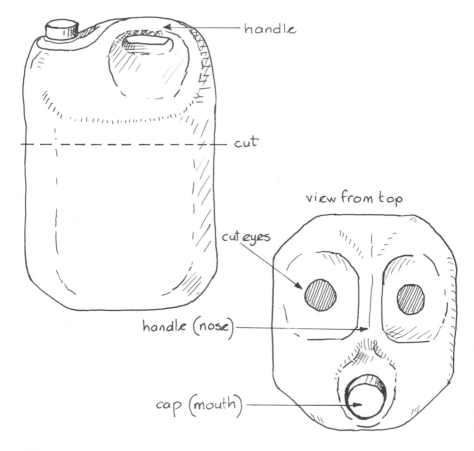

handle

cut

view from top

cut eyes

handle (nose)

cap (mouth)

Wash the container tops thoroughly and cut out the eyes for the children in the right places. Make up some powder paint with some P.V.A. glue (this will cover sufficiently and not peel off as powder paint alone will do). The children can then paint their masks and when the paint is dry, stick on bits of collage (buttons, foil, seeds and so on).

These masks are very strong and children love making them. I call them tribal masks because they are bright and colourful, but also a little menacing like warpaint. Attach with wide elastic, stapled either side of the mask. Or you could fasten on a length of dowelling so the child can hold the mask up to his or her face. Some containers already have handles on the sides for the children to hold under their chins.

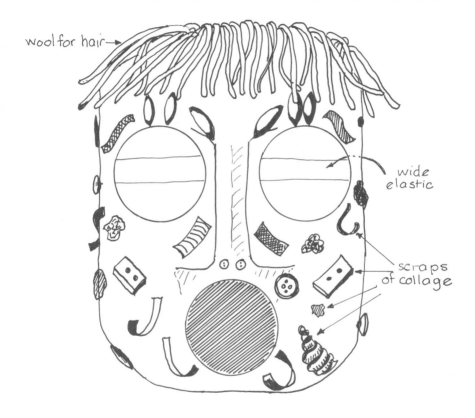

wool for hair→

wide elastic

scraps of collage

Hats

All measurements for hats and masks will vary for different ages.

When fastening with staples, make sure you staple from the inside so the sharp ends are on the outside and not going to scratch the child's face.

Indian headdresses

Make a template of an oblong long enough to go round a child's head and wide enough to form a band (approx 60 × 6 cm) and ask the children to draw round it on to stiff paper or card. They then use bright felt tip pens to make patterns along the band. Make a template for feathers which the children also draw round, cut out and colour. Fix the feathers to the back of the band once it has been bent round to fit the child's head and fastened with staples. It's fun to have an American 'Indian day' and use some face paints to finish off the outfit.

Father Christmas hat

Get the children to cut an oblong of red tissue paper each and a band of plain paper. They then stick the longest edge of the tissue on to the length of band (therefore these measurements should be the same) and then stick cotton wool over this along the edge of the hat. When it is dry, bend round to fit the child's head and staple; then gather the back up to form a cap, glue and stick on a blob of cotton wool, for a pom-pom (this also hides the join). Make a Father Christmas mask and sack to complete the look.

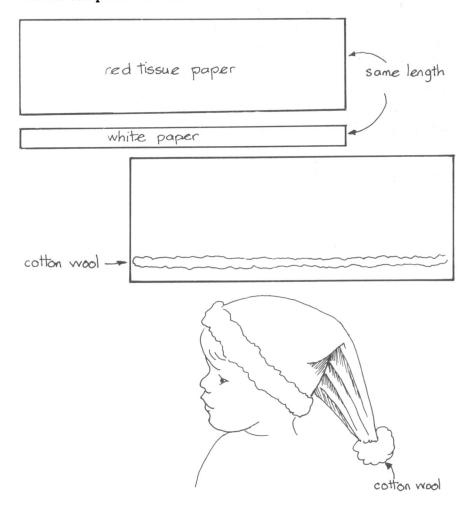

Crown

Using an oblong band of card draw a serrated edge along the top half and ask the children to cut on the line. Then they can decorate with pieces of shiny foil or sticky paper or paint. Bend round the head and fasten with staples.

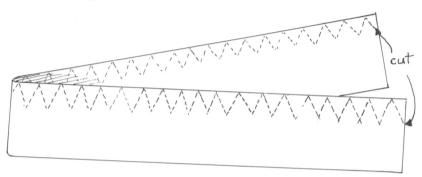

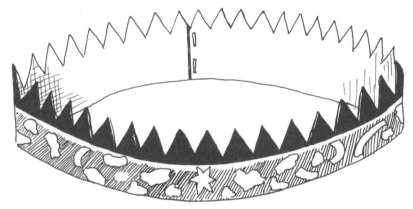

Witch's hat

Draw a large circle from black sugar paper and ask the child to cut into the centre. Overlap the two edges to form a cone and staple. Then cut a smaller circle. Fold it in half to make it easier for the child and cut out the middle of this to form a rim. Decorate with silver stars, cats, bits of paper and so on.

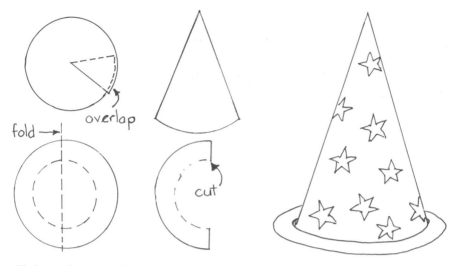

fold →

overlap

cut

Fringed party hat

The children make headbands as before in Indian Headdress. Then ask each child to cut a deeper oblong (60 × 40 cms) from either coloured foil or crepe paper. They then paste along the headband and stick it firmly to the bottom edge of the large oblong – this strengthens the base of the hat. Whilst that end is drying, you draw several short lines down from the other end and ask the child to cut down these forming a fringe. When dry bend the hat carefully round the child's head and fix, then gather the fringed top together and tie with a piece of cotton.

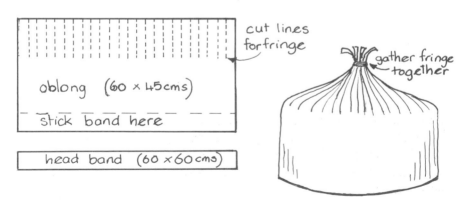

cut lines for fringe

oblong (60 × 45cms)

stick band here

head band (60 × 60cms)

gather fringe together

Chef's or Cook's Hat

The children again make a headband from white card and a large oblong (60 × 35 cms approx) from white crepe paper. They stick the band along the bottom of the white crepe as before to strengthen the hat. Why dry fold the hat round the child's head and fasten Carefully fold and shape the top edges in together to the middle and keep together with a large blob of PVA glue. You may need to secure on the inside with sticky tape.

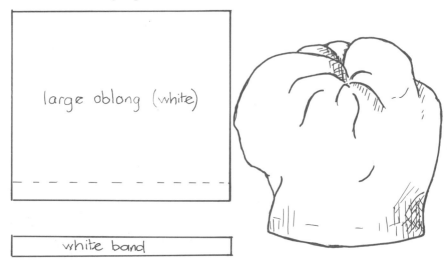

large oblong (white)

white band

Quick Sun-Hat

If you need an emergency hat for a sun-baked child on the beach then you could use this simple method:

Grab dad's newspaper and pull off a whole sheet. Lay it on the ground and fold it towards you using the fold already there.

Then fold the top right-hand corner down towards the centre bottom, to form a diagonal line and repeat with the top left-hand corner to form a sort of triangle. (a) Then fold up one bottom edge to form a rim and turn the hat over to turn up the other edge. (b) This should keep the hat together, and there you are. (c) Of course, if making as a group activity the children could paint the newspaper, or make from plain paper to decorate as they wish.

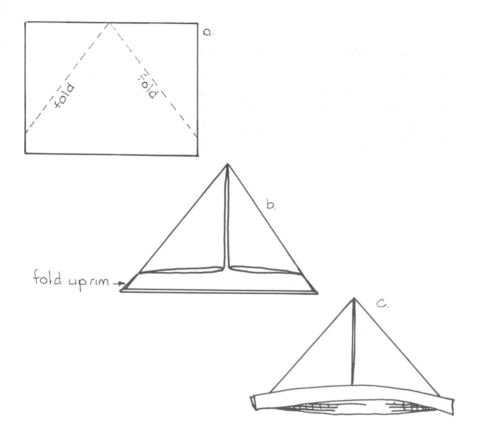

A Lady's Bonnet

Cut and open out a finished cereal packet. (a) Then make a template of an oblong about 12 × 40 cms – long enough to go over the child's hand ear to ear. Each child then lays the template on to the plain side of the cereal packet, across the whole width so the side panel is in the middle. (b) This is important as the side panel ends up sitting on top of the child's head and the bonnet folds easily round. They then draw round and cut out the shape, you should be able to get 3 hats from 1 large cereal packet. The child then decorates the bonnet in any way she chooses, e.g., sticking on light collage, magazine pictures or pictures cut from greeting cards. (c) Finally, punch a hole either end of the hat and thread a piece of pretty ribbon or braid through each. The child wears the hat over the top of her head and tied under her chin, like a bonnet. (d) Although I've called it 'A Lady's Bonnet', of course there should be nothing stopping the boys making one if they want it.

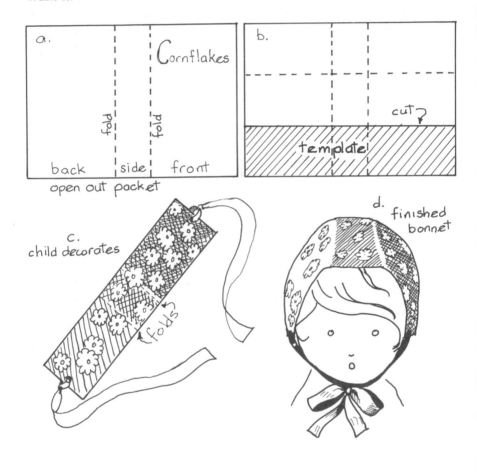

a. Cornflakes

fold fold

back side front

open out packet

b. cut

template

c. child decorates

folds

d. finished bonnet

Mobiles

Mobiles suspended on strong thread from the ceiling will move with the air currents in the room. The frames can be made in many ways. If working in a school, you have access to the large hoops used for P.E., perhaps slightly bent ones or broken ones which can be rejoined. Cover a hoop with strips of crepe paper wound round it and tie four lengths of wool from the circumference of the hoop to the middle. Tie these together on to one long piece of wool to suspend from ceiling.

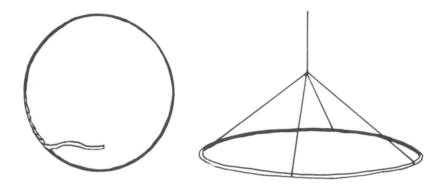

Alternatively, snip the hook off a wire coat hanger with wire cutters. Slot it inside another coat hanger to form a star and tie the two firmly at the hook. Cover with strips of crepe paper as above.

You may be able to think of many other ways of making mobile frames, but remember they should be sturdy: then they can stay up permanently while you change only whatever has been made to hang from them. Small children will not appreciate anything too high so hang mobiles just above reaching level, even if adults tend to crash into them!

Birds

Make a template of a bird for the children to draw round and cut out. Ask them to colour *both sides* brown, or stick on curled pieces of tissue for feathers. Wings can be made with concertina paper (that is, folded as you would make a fan). Bend the concertina in the middle and push through a slit in the bird's body.

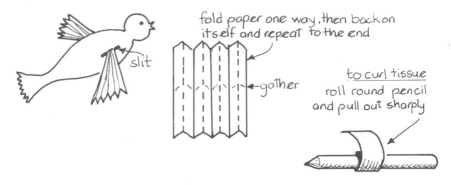

You can vary the birds' shapes and colouring to make robins for Christmas or chicks for Easter.

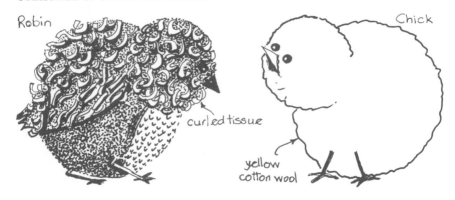

Butterflies

Make as described on page 24 in the chapter on painting. Don't forget a piece of straw threaded through between the wings will help to stop them dropping.

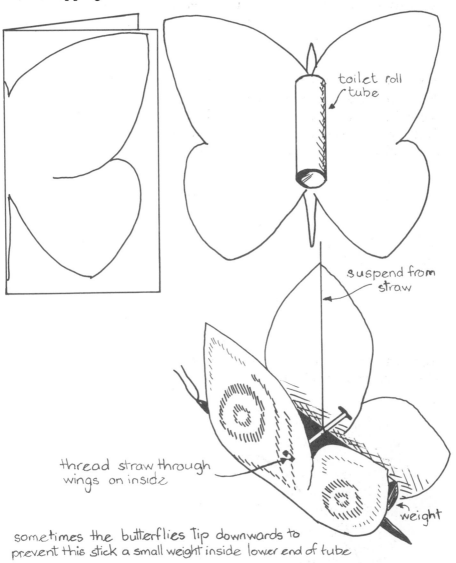

toilet roll tube

suspend from straw

thread straw through wings on inside

weight

sometimes the butterflies tip downwards to prevent this stick a small weight inside lower end of tube

Fish

Draw a simple template of a fish as shown and ask the children to cut out two of these shapes from wallpaper (remember to reverse the wallpaper so the pattern side matches). Place the two fish on top of one another and staple all the way round the edge, leaving a gap large enough for the child to stuff with screwed-up newspaper. When it is full, close the gap with staples and then the child can stick on shiny foil pieces for scales and milk bottle tops for an eyes.

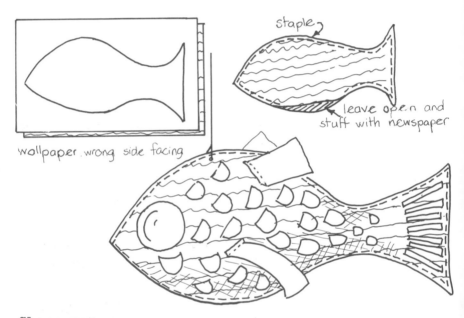

wallpaper wrong side facing

staple

leave open and stuff with newspaper

Shape men

Example: Mr Circle. The children can draw round large circular objects, such as washing-up bowls, on to strong card to make the heads and bodies. Margarine tubs can be used for arms and legs. Then the children can stick on features and clothes, remembering to keep as much as possible circular; a bright spotty fabric could be used for the shirt, and curtain rings or buttons for hair. Finally, when everything is dry, assemble each circle separately with paper fasteners so the character is bendable. Suspend from the mobile with long strings from Mr Circle's head and arms.

This can be used in a project on shape, and other characters can be easily made on the same principle, for example, Mr Square, Mr Triangle, Mr Oblong (or Mr Rectangle).

Weather

Using perhaps three or four hoops, a lovely project can be produced on different forms of weather:

Snow The children can stick blobs of cotton wool on to lengths of string around one hoop, and make snowflakes with the children to hang in between – see page 38.

Rain Transform another hoop into an umbrella by wrapping tissue paper over the top and suspending cut pieces of sellophane at intervals down clear or white string (many parcels are wrapped with this type of string now). The transparency looks like raindrops.

Sun The children can draw round a large circular object and cut it out. Then they can paint a lovely bright sun. If you have time collect many different pieces of yellow fabric (in various shades and patterns) and cut them into rough squares; if the children are older they may be able to cut the fabric themselves. Then they stick a collage of yellow on the sun shape. The children can also draw, cut and paint yellow triangles to go round the edge of the circle for the sun's rays.

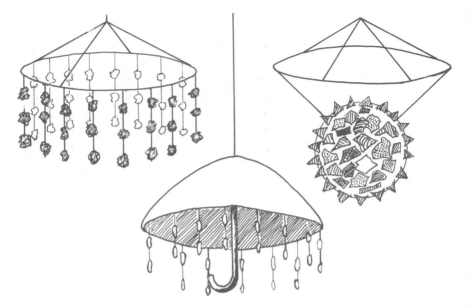

Lambs

Make a template of a bouncing spring lamb and ask the children to draw round it on to white card and cut it out. Then they can stick cotton wool on both sides, and bright black eyes made from gummed paper.

Frogs

Make as described in the section on Models on page 50, but remember to cover both sides. The polystyrene is very strong and frogs made from it hang beautifully.

Chicks

Make a template by cutting round two circles drawn from a large margarine tub (for the chick's body) and a small margarine tub (for the head). The children can then draw round the templates on to yellow card and cut out. Either stick on yellow cotton wool, or white cotton wool dampened and flicked with yellow powder paint (not made-up). Cut a beak and feet from orange paper. Suspend four chicks from a mobile and in between hang a half of a broken eggshell below the chicks to look as if they have just hatched out.

Bee

Ask the children to paint a toilet roll yellow and, when it is dry, carefully to paint on black stripes; for young children who may find this difficult, you could stick on strips of black gummed paper which they have cut out. They can then draw a head as shown, cut it out, and stick it on to the toilet roll each side. Wings can be made from paper and the middle of each cut out so the children can stick in a small piece of coloured tissue paper. This gives the appearance of the fine transparent wings a bee has and is very effective when light shines through it.

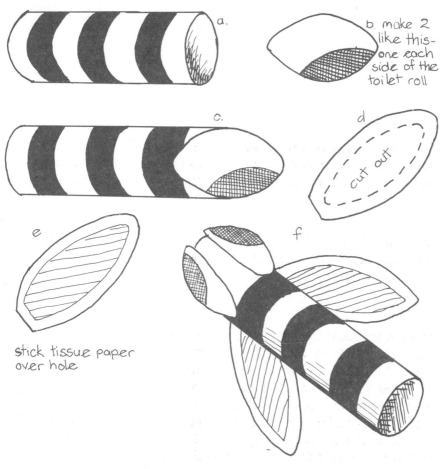

a.

b. make 2 like this- one each side of the toilet roll

c.

d cut out

e

stick tissue paper over hole

f

Flowers

Daffodils 1

Ask the children to cut a segment from a yellow plastic eggbox (they may need help with this) or to paint a cardboard one yellow. From a petal template that you have made, the children can draw and cut out six paper petals and colour them yellow. Fasten the petals at the back of the daffodil's trumpet (the egg segment) and fill the middle of flower with a screwed-up piece of yellow tissue paper. A stem can be made from a straw painted green if the daffodil is to be displayed on the wall or on a card (ideal for Mother's Day or Easter). If the daffodil is to be held, use a toilet roll tube painted green and fastened firmly to the back of the flower.

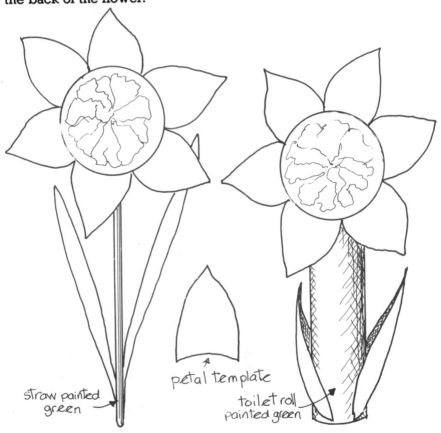

straw painted green

petal template

toilet roll painted green

Daffodils 2

The children paint toilet rolls green, for the stem. Then for each flower they can cut out two segments from a yellow polystyrene egg box. Draw four lines down one of the segments which the children then cut. Fix the other segment inside this one with a paper fastener. Then poke the fastener through the top of the toilet roll and open out the pins inside. The children can then draw and cut out two leaves from green gummed paper, lick the backs and stick them on at the bottom of the flower.

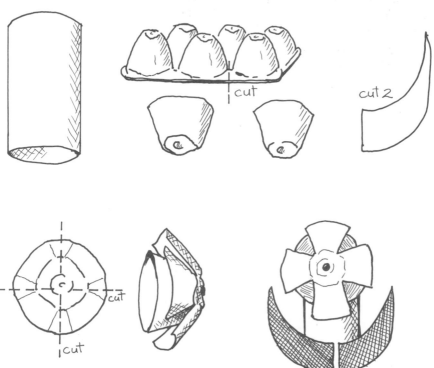

Assorted

This is a very simple, quick method for making paper flowers. Cut several squares of coloured tissue paper in various sizes (12 cms, 8 cms and 5 cms); then fold each square in half, and half again. Then fold diagonally and draw a heart shape at the wide end. The children can cut on the line and open up the flower. If they choose three different colours of three different sizes of squares and cut each size the same, the petals can be assembled with large ones at the bottom, middle size next, and smallest on the top. Only a dab of glue is needed in the middle of each petal to hold it in place. Ideal for pictures and cards or, if fixed on a stick, the flowers can be held.

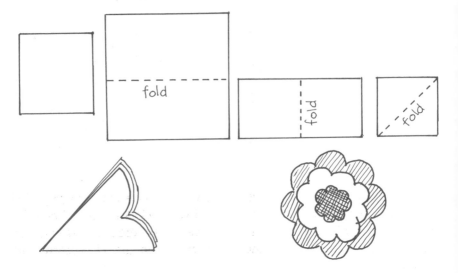

Carnations

A similar method to above, but a softer effect is achieved if household tissues are used. Fold as before and trim the edges with pinking shears. Gather several tissues together by pinching in the middle at the back and fasten by twisting round to form a stem. Cover the stem with silver foil. Ideal for a wedding. Older children may be able to edge the carnation carefully with felt tip pens to finish them off really well.

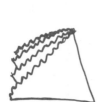

Wallpaper flowers

Let the children sort through wallpaper sample books and find flowery wallpaper. Help them to cut out the flowers by drawing round them with a pencil. Young children in particular find it difficult to judge where to cut to remove just one thing from a picture, so until they acquire this skill a pencil line to cut on helps greatly.

Bluebells

Squares of approximately 5 cm are cut from blue tissue paper. Roll them round a pencil and slide off, holding the base firmly. Stick the base together with a dab of glue. Make several of these tubes and then they can be stuck on to long thin stems made from drinking straws and painted.

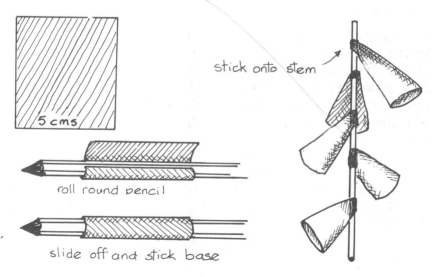

5 cms

roll round pencil

slide off and stick base

stick onto stem

Bubble flowers

Prepare a bubble painting activity as described on page 19. When the pictures are dry, the children can carefully cut round the shapes to form flowers. These are lovely attached to green stems for friezes.

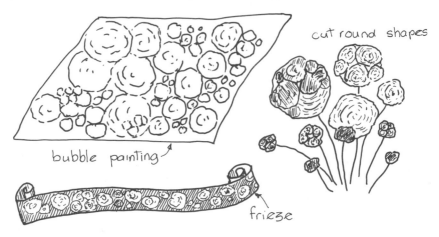

cut round shapes

bubble painting

frieze

Star flowers

Very quick and simple to make. Make a template of a star for the children to use: the best way to get an equal star is to draw a triangle and then draw another one on top of it but upside down. Cut round the edge of the completed shape as shown.

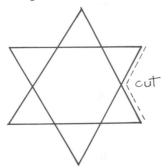

cut

The children can draw round this template, colour with bright felt tips and cut out. Then make a hole in the centre of the flower and push it on to a rolled up oblong of green card or crepe paper.

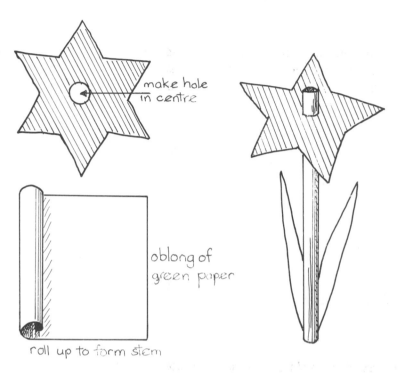

make hole in centre

oblong of green paper

roll up to form stem

Eggbox flowers

Collect plastic eggboxes in any colour, or the children can paint cardboard ones in bright colours. Stick on to stems from sticks or paper and add leaves.

Flower pictures

Using garden catalogues, ask the children carefully to cut out large flowers. These can then be used for a frieze or cards.

Stained glass flowers

As described in the cutting and sticking section, page 36.

Roses

Make a template. Cut three triangles (about 8 cm each side) from red tissue, or the children may find red sugar paper easier to cut.

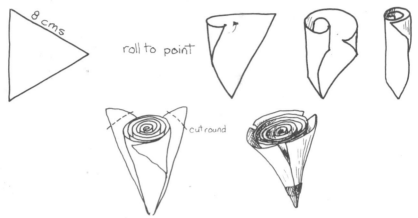

Roll the first triangle from the edge to the point and then roll the remaining two triangles round the first, to form a tight bud.

The children cut three more triangles slightly smaller (using a second template). Bend up and place round the bud so they stick out to form petals.

Cut off the points to a curve and bend outwards.

Pinch the base and staple or sellotape together.

Quite fiddly for very young children.

Quick and easy flowers

The children draw round a yoghurt carton and cut two circles from different coloured tissue paper. A blob of glue in the centre will fasten the two together. Pinch the middle and twist it round to form a stem. The flowers can be stuck on to hats for Easter bonnets, or on to pictures and cards gathered in bunches.

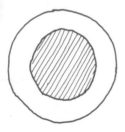